THE SPOTTED OWL

Alvin, Virginia, and Robert Silverstein
THE MILLBROOK PRESS, BROOKFIELD, CONNECTICUT

Cover photograph courtesy of © Art Wolfe Inc., Seattle
Photographs courtesy of USDA Forest Service, Pacific Northwest
Region: pp. 8, 11, 20, 22; Art Wolfe Inc.: pp. 14, 18, 41, 44, 53;
USDA Forest Service, Pacific Southwest Region: p. 16; USDA Forest
Service, Washington, D.C.: pp. 25 (Curt Given), 27, 56 (both, Ken
Hammond); AP/Wide World: p. 32; Tom Reese, Seattle Times: pp. 34,
37; Barry Wong, Seattle Times: p.40; Betty Udesen, Seattle Times:
p. 46; Reuters/Bettmann: p. 49. Map by Joe Le Monnier

Library of Congress Cataloging-in-Publication Data
Silverstein, Alvin.
The spotted owl / by Alvin, Virginia, and Robert Silverstein.
    p.   cm.—(Endangered in America)
Includes bibliographical references (p.   ) and index.
Summary: Describes the three types of spotted owls with
emphasis on the northern spotted owl.
ISBN 1-56294-415-0 (lib. bdg.)
1. Spotted owl—North America—Juvenile literature.   2. Endangered
species—Northwest, Pacific—Juvenile literature.   3. Birds,
Protection of—Northwest, Pacific—Juvenile literature.   4. Lumber
trade—Northwest, Pacific—Juvenile literature.   [1. Spotted owl.
2. Endangered species.   3. Birds—Protection.   4. Old growth
forests.   5. Lumber and lumbering.]   I. Silverstein, Virginia B.
II. Silverstein, Robert A.   III. Title.   IV. Series: Silverstein,
Alvin. Endangered in America.
QL696.S83S55   1994   333.95'8—dc20   93-42624   CIP   AC

Published by The Millbrook Press
2 Old New Milford Road, Brookfield, Connecticut 06804

The authors would like to thank Christine Sheppard, Curator of Ornithology at the NYZS International Wildlife Conservation Park/Bronx Zoo, for her careful reading of the manuscript and her many helpful comments and suggestions.

Thanks also to Jack Ward Thomas of the Forest Service, Erran Seaman of the National Park Service, and all the others who generously shared information and insights about the spotted owl and the fight to save it.

CONTENTS

People Versus Owls?
9

The Spotted Owl
13

Studying Spotted Owls
24

The Fight for the Spotted Owl
30

The Debate Continues
36

The Broader Picture
48

Notes 55
Facts About the Spotted Owl 57
Further Reading 58
Organizations to Contact 59
Index 61

The northern spotted owl has become the focus of a fierce debate
between business and environmental groups.

PEOPLE VERSUS OWLS?

If you travel in logging country in Oregon and Washington, you are likely to see bumper stickers reading, "I Love Spotted Owls—For Lunch" or "Save A Logger—Shoot an Owl." You may even see people wearing "I Love spotted owls . . . fried" T-shirts.

Loggers don't really hate spotted owls, but it seems to them that the government is placing more importance on owls than on people's jobs and way of life. For many years, logging communities have depended on the business of cutting trees and making them into thousands of different products we use. Lumber is used for building houses and making furniture. Wood pulp is used for the paper we write on, the newspapers and books we read, and even toilet paper.

Spotted owls live in special forests called *old-growth forests* in the Pacific Northwest. These forests provide the kind of homes and living conditions the owls need. The trees in these woods are big and old. Most are hundreds of years old; some have been growing for a thousand years. When settlers first came to the West, there were a lot more old-growth forests than there are today. Many have been cut down to provide the timber for building materials and other products.

The numbers of spotted owls have been decreasing as loggers cut down more of the woods in which they live. Scientists are worried that these owls might become extinct if people continue to cut down old-growth forests. Then there wouldn't be any northern spotted owls left in the world.

That's where the problem is. Environmentalists want logging to stop in old-growth forests, to protect the spotted owl and the thousands of other creatures that live there. The timber industry says that regulations preventing them from cutting these trees are causing many people to lose their jobs. People have been arguing about this "owl versus jobs" question for many years. But recently it has grown to a national concern.

AN ECOSYSTEM IN DANGER

The ancient forests make up an *ecosystem* in which an intricate web of life is carefully balanced. The spotted owl has an important role in this delicate balance, helping to keep the numbers of small leaf- and seed-eating animals in check.

Biologists call the spotted owl an "indicator species" and compare it to the canaries that miners once brought with them into the mines where they worked. Canaries are very sensitive to the poisonous gases that are sometimes found in underground mines. So a canary was like an early warning system: If it died, the miners knew the levels of poisonous gases were getting dangerous.

Similarly, spotted owls are an early warning signal of damage to the ecosystem. These owls feed on squirrels, mice, and other small animals that eat seeds and nuts of forest trees and fungi growing on fallen trees and other decaying matter. When the forest ecosystem is healthy, the seeds and fungi are plentiful, and so are the small mammals that feed on them. If the numbers of small mammals decrease, there is less food for spotted owls, and fewer of them survive. Spotted owls are a good indicator species because they are easier to observe and count than the small

Ancient Forests

THE NAME "ancient forests" was coined in 1988 by a conservation group called the Oregon Natural Resources Council, to describe old-growth forests. These are areas that have never been exposed to cutting. Some California redwoods and sequoias have been living since the time of the Roman Empire. But the term "old growth" is usually used for trees at least 200 years old, with trunks at least 32 inches (80 centimeters) in diameter. Old-growth forests help to regulate the climate, maintain water levels, prevent flooding, clean the air, and enrich the soil, in addition to being the home of a complex community of plants and animals. Scientists still have much to learn about how all these forest dwellers interact.

Some trees in old-growth forests are hundreds of years old.

mammals that scurry about among the forest litter. They are also sensitive to changes in the ecosystem because they need a large hunting territory to catch enough food to survive. Scientists have found that, with extensive logging, the number of spotted owls is decreasing, and the ancient forest ecosystem is dying.

When settlers first came to the West, there were at least 17 million acres (7 million hectares) of old-growth forests in Oregon and Washington. Now estimates of the amount left range from 8 to 30 percent of that amount. (Environmentalists claim there is very little left; the timber industry supports the higher estimate.)

About half of the land in the West is owned by the government. The Department of the Interior oversees several federal agencies that manage this land. Some of it is preserved in national parks and national forest wildernesses. Some is leased to ranchers for cattle to graze. Some is mined. Timber from national forests is sold to loggers. Usually the loggers pay much less to use government land than the current rate for privately owned land. So our government has been actively promoting the *use* of timber resources rather than their conservation. But, more and more, people have been questioning this policy.

The spotted owl controversy is focused on about 3 million acres (1.2 million hectares) of old-growth trees on land managed by the Forest Service and the Bureau of Land Management. The timber industry wants to be able to harvest timber on this land. Environmentalists want to preserve it and the spotted owls and other wildlife that live there.

Many people on both sides of the debate are surprised that such a small bird could cause so much fuss. But the spotted owl has helped to bring the importance of conserving the nation's wilderness and wildlife into the public spotlight. It is helping people to see the need to work at compromises that consider not only economic benefits for people but the well-being of wildlife, too. Progress is being made in helping to solve the owl-versus-jobs problem, but it is likely that the debate will continue.

THE SPOTTED OWL

Owls are among the most familiar birds, known from many popular stories and fables. Yet, most people have never seen a real, live owl (except in zoos). Most owls hunt at night, when most people are asleep. Perhaps they hear an owl's hooting call, a spooky sound in the dark. During the day, owls usually rest hidden in their nests high in trees.

Owls have big heads and short, plump bodies, thickly covered with feathers. The fluffy body and big round eyes may seem "cute," but real owls are hardly cuddly. They are fierce hunters that can catch a small animal or bird with sharp-clawed feet and rip it apart or swallow it whole. With large, powerful wings they can soar and swoop. Soft, fluffy feathers at the ends of their wings muffle the flapping sounds and allow owls to fly silently. That is an advantage when owls hunt; an owl can swoop down without warning to catch its prey.

An owl's big eyes can see things clearly, even at night, but hunting owls depend even more on their keen hearing. Tightly packed rows of stiff feathers around an owl's eyes form a pattern called the facial disk that acts as a sort of sound funnel, directing sounds to the owl's ears. (Some owls have tufts of feathers on their heads, which stick up like a cat's ears. But the owl's real ears are on the sides of its head, hidden under feathers.) An owl can locate a mouse in total darkness just from the tiny sounds it makes moving through the leaves on the forest floor.

A northern spotted owl closes in on its prey, a field mouse.

THREE TYPES OF SPOTTED OWLS

There are more than a hundred different kinds of owls, which live in practically all parts of the world. Each plays an important role in the balance of nature in the area where it lives.

The spotted owl is a medium-sized owl, from 16 to 19 inches (40 to 48 centimeters) long. As with most owls, female spotted owls are larger than the males. Males weigh up to about 1.5 pounds (0.7 kilogram); females are slightly heavier.

Spotted owls are a rich, chocolate-brown color. Their name comes from the white spots found on the top of the head and back of the neck. The underside of the owl's body is rusty brown, with darker crossbars and white spots and dashes. The spotted owl has big dark gray-brown eyes and a pale yellow bill. Its head is round, without the "horns," or ear tufts, that some owls have. The feathers surrounding the eyes are a pale buff against the darker reddish brown of the sides and top of the head.

The spotted owl is related to the barred owls (often called hoot owls) that live on the East Coast. (Like spotted owls, barred owls' feathers have a pattern of dark crossbars against a lighter background.) The scientific name for spotted owls is *Strix occidentalis*.

The "job-versus-owl" debate has focused on the northern spotted owl (*Strix occidentalis caurina*). But there are also two other types of spotted owls. The California spotted owl (*Strix occidentalis occidentalis*) is very closely related to the northern spotted owl. The Mexican spotted owl (*Strix occidentalis lucida*) is their cousin to the south. Both these owls are also threatened by logging in their natural habitat.

Spotted owls make several different kinds of sounds. The main one is a series of three to five booming, high-pitched hoots: "ow-ow-ow-ow-ow." Some people think that this hoot sounds like a barking dog. When

California spotted owls like this one are also threatened by logging.

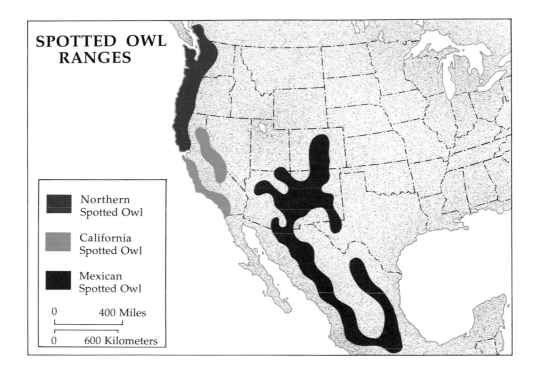

SPOTTED OWL
RANGES

Northern
Spotted Owl

California
Spotted Owl

Mexican
Spotted Owl

0   400 Miles

0   600 Kilometers

spotted owls are disturbed in their nest they may make a low, rising whistle. Sometimes they may make dovelike hoots, too. Spotted owls are graceful in flight, but moving along a tree branch they have a parrotlike walk.

Spotted owls are found in western North America from southwestern British Columbia down to central Mexico. Northern spotted owls range from northern California up through Oregon and Washington into British Columbia. The ancient forests where they live are mostly made up of redwood, hemlock, and Douglas fir. The trees are very big, and their trunks often have deep holes, formed by disease and decay. These holes are ideal, sheltered places for the owls to nest in. Except under special conditions, the owls are unable to settle in new plantations of trees.

An ancient, moss-covered evergreen branch makes a
perfect perch for a young northern spotted owl.

Ancient forests contain many tall trees, up to 200 feet (60 meters) high, as well as smaller young trees growing up below the leaf canopy of the older trees. These forests provide spotted owls with a two-level environment that allows them to survive through cold winters and hot summers. During the cold season, the spotted owl roosts in the broken tops of old trees (the overstory), where the warmth of the sun helps to keep its body temperature stable. (Its thick, fluffy feathers act like a blanket, holding in heat.) The canopy catches the heavy winter snows, keeping the forest floor clear enough for small animals to find food and, in turn, be prey for hunting owls. During the warm summer months, the owl spends much of its time roosting in smaller trees, such as Pacific yews, in the shadier forest understory, sheltered from the hot sun.

WHAT DO SPOTTED OWLS EAT?

Like most owls, spotted owls are nocturnal; they rarely move about during the day unless they are disturbed. At night they hunt for flying squirrels, young snowshoe hares, pocket gophers, deer mice, wood rats, bats, shrews, moles, small birds such as Steller's jays, small owls, frogs, and insects such as crickets, cockroaches, and beetles. (One study found that a typical spotted owl in the central Cascade Mountains ate 235 flying squirrels a year, and that was about half of its total diet.)

Spotted owls are powerful hunters. Studies have found that nesting pairs hunt more large mammals and fewer small ones than those that are not nesting. If they catch more than they need, they hide the extra food to eat later.

When hunting, a spotted owl perches quietly, watching carefully for prey. When it sees or hears something, it swoops down silently and snatches up the unlucky victim in its claws. Two of the toes on each foot point forward and the other two point backward. The owl can spread its toes wide to seize its prey. When it is taking food home to the nest, though, it holds the dead prey in its beak.

Like other owls, the spotted owl can turn its head in
a full half-circle, to see what's directly behind it.

A SPOTTED OWL'S LIFE CYCLE

Spotted owls may live for 15 years in the wild, but they do not begin reproducing until their third year. Spotted owls often mate for life. But during the winter the pair separates, and each lives alone. They return to the same nest each spring. Usually, a pair of spotted owls does not bother to build a nest. They use an abandoned hawk nest instead, or they settle down in a cup-shaped hole in a broken tree. Rotting wood and leaf litter form a cushion at the bottom of the nest; as the years go by, powdered bones and fur of their prey add to the cushion.

Spotted owls do not usually breed every year. On the average, they hatch owlets every other year. Usually two eggs are laid, but sometimes there is only one, and as many as four have been recorded in nests of California spotted owls. The female sits on the eggs nearly all the time, and her mate brings food to her. When the eggs hatch in April or May, the male continues to bring food for the female and the young for another two weeks, until the female is ready to spend some of her time hunting, too.

Baby spotted owlets are covered with white down. Their eyes open after five to nine days. By ten to twenty days, pale brown feathers start to grow in. By 34 to 36 days, the owlets may begin short, awkward flights. Often, spotted owlets leave the nest before they are able to fly well. Some of them simply fall out, but scientists believe that others are trying to escape from bloodsucking flies that are attracted to the messy litter in the nest. Most of the young owlets that leave the nest too early are killed by the fall, or eaten by predators. Those that survive may spend a week or two on the ground until they have enough feathers to fly. They use the sharp talons on their toes to climb trees and hold on to the trunk with their wings when they get tired. Their parents continue to feed them until they are able to fly and hunt on their own.

Feathers have begun to replace down on this pair of northern spotted owlets.

A few weeks after they have begun to fly, the owlets are able to tear up prey themselves. By midsummer they have learned to catch crawling insects, and by September they are usually able to hunt for small rodents.

THE SPOTTED OWL POPULATION IS DECLINING

Scientists have spent two decades searching for spotted owl nests. During that time, the spotted owl population counts have actually been going up—even while the real numbers have been decreasing—simply because so many people have been looking for the owls, and finding them in places that had not been studied before. Most current estimates of the number of spotted owls remaining range from 3,000 to 5,000 pairs. That may seem like a lot of owls, but in areas that have been studied intensively over a period of years, the numbers have been decreasing by nearly 1 percent a year.

The struggle for survival is difficult for most creatures, and owls are no exception. Many owlets die before they can reproduce. In one study, 89 percent of the owlets died before they left the nest. In another study, a third of the owlets that survived to go out on their own were dead by the end of their first summer. Some young owls were killed by predators such as great horned owls. Others were unable to find enough to eat. Not only has the owls' habitat been shrinking, but a new problem has recently been added. Barred owls have been spreading westward. By 1970, they reached the West Coast, and they began competing with spotted owls for prey.

After many studies had been conducted, researchers concluded that the spotted owl could survive in its natural habitat, in spite of the high mortality rate of owlets. But it could not survive in areas where a lot of logging has taken place. This changes the ecosystem too much, and the owls cannot breed or find enough food to survive.

STUDYING SPOTTED OWLS

Scientists first discovered the spotted owl in March 1858. A naturalist came across one while traveling in the southern Sierra Nevadas. The next one wasn't spotted until 1872, in Arizona. When early naturalists "studied" spotted owls, they usually brought back killed specimens, and took the eggs from their nests. Modern scientists study living spotted owls in their natural habitat.

Because spotted owls come out only at night and live deep within ancient pine forests, not many people have ever seen one. But once found, they are very easy to observe, because they are remarkably unafraid of people. The spotted owl has been described as both one of the tamest and one of the stupidest owls. A spotted owl will just sit in its nest and watch people even a few inches away.

SPOTTING SPOTTED OWLS

In 1968, Eric Forsman, a 28-year-old biology student at Oregon State University in Corvallis, was working for the Forest Service over the summer. One evening, while alone at his post deep in the woods, he heard an odd barking sound. Having read a lot about owls, he realized it

A U.S. Forest Service biologist has a close encounter with a spotted owl.
The owls often allow people to come very near.

was probably a spotted owl, and he hooted back. The owl answered him. Forsman hooted again. Then, unexpectedly, the owl flew down and landed nearby, staring up at the young biologist. The owl seemed to be completely unafraid of him. Forsman was excited. Until then, spotted owls had been seen only twenty-five times in the whole history of the Pacific Northwest.

Forsman continued observing spotted owls until he was drafted into military service in 1970. When he returned two years later, he started working on a master's degree on the spotted owl at Oregon State University. Over the next two decades, he and dozens of other biologists spent thousands of hours searching for spotted owls by hooting to them and listening for a reply. They recorded more than a dozen different calls.

The wildlife biologists would walk or drive down forest trails at night, stopping every hundred yards or so to hoot, or play a recording of a spotted owl hooting. They listened carefully for an owl to call back. If one did, they returned to that site in the daylight. Again they would call the owl to try to get it to come to the ground.

To lure the owl, a mouse on a leash was tied to a log. The owl would swoop down and grab the mouse in its sharp claws and then head back to the nest. The scientists would then run as fast as they could across the rough terrain to locate the nest. If the owl's nest was too far away, they would often lose it and have to try again. But many nests were mapped in this way. Researchers also tracked the owls by catching them and strapping little radio transmitters onto their backs. The scientists could track the owls by the radio signals to discover their hunting habits.

The biologists also studied owl pellets. When owls eat, they swallow their prey whole. The bones and fur or feathers are not digested but are coughed up in pellets. Researchers can tell what types of prey make up the owl's diet by looking at what kinds of bones, fur, and other animal remains these pellets contain.

Biologists examine a captured owl and record information about it before releasing it.

As more researchers joined in spotted owl mapping, the search widened from central Oregon up to Washington and down into the California redwoods. By 1992, the Forest Service count was 3,602 pairs of spotted owls, with 671 in Washington, 1,971 in Oregon, and 960 pairs in California.

THE NEED FOR OLD GROWTH

One of the first things the scientists noticed while mapping spotted owl nests was that these owls were found only where there were untouched old-growth trees. When scientists monitored radio-tagged owls, they saw that the owls flew over large areas of smaller trees to find the few surviving old-growth areas to roost in.

Researchers speculated on why spotted owls tend to roost in old-growth forests. According to one guess, it was because that's where flying squirrels, their favorite prey, live. Another idea was that the owls preferred nesting in the tops of big old trees. Tree trunks were bigger and trees were farther apart in the old-growth forests, so the owls had more room to fly.

Timber industry scientists have found a few spotted owls in second-growth forests. Industry spokespeople have used this discovery as the basis for arguing that environmentalists are exaggerating the need for old-growth trees. They claim that the owl could adapt to other habitats. But wildlife biologists point out that spotted owls are found in other habitats only very rarely, under special conditions that are not present in most second-growth woods.

It is the spotted owls' need for old-growth forests that has sparked the battle between environmentalists, who want to save the ancient forests, and the timber industry, which wants to continue to harvest this natural resource.

THE FIGHT FOR THE SPOTTED OWL

In 1972, while still a graduate student in Corvallis, Oregon, Eric Forsman found three spotted owl nests in the city's 10,000 acre (400-hectare) watershed. When he learned that 100 acres (40 hectares) of trees near one of the spotted owl nests were to be cut down, he wrote several times to the city's water supervisor, pointing out the danger to the spotted owls that lived there.

Actually, the Watershed Study Committee had decided to increase the number of trees cut because there were a lot of decayed and diseased trees and because sale of the timber would provide the city with income. No one realized at the time that just this kind of conflict concerning the spotted owl would come up again and again, only on a much bigger scale.

Forsman wrote letters to the editor, gave talks for the local Audubon Society, and sent information about the spotted owl to the Forest Service and Bureau of Land Management. He became an authority. When Congress passed the Endangered Species Act of 1973, the spotted owl was included in the list of potentially endangered species.

THE ENDANGERED SPECIES ACT

The Endangered Species Act of 1973 (ESA) was built on several earlier laws, dating from 1900, which were designed to protect American wildlife that was threatened with extinction. The act forbids any action funded, authorized, or carried out by federal agencies that would threaten the survival of endangered species. It also forbids the "taking" of any endangered species (which means harming, killing, or removing from its habitat), on both federal and private lands.

The law has provisions for adding more species to the list of endangered species if needed, and removing species from the list if they are later considered out of danger. All decisions on the listing and delisting of species must be made solely on the basis of science, without considering economic consequences such as a loss of jobs or land value.

The ESA thus declared that the survival of animal and plant species was more important than the financial benefits that developing an area could bring. But many endangered species are still unprotected. Each year the U.S. Fish and Wildlife Service (FWS) is given only enough money to determine whether or not about 50 species are endangered. By 1993, about 600 U.S. species had been listed as endangered or threatened, but scientists believed that there were probably 3,000 more in jeopardy.

The Fish and Wildlife Service was supposed to develop recovery plans for the endangered species, including ways to protect their habitat or even to breed them in captivity to restore their numbers. But without enough funding, the FWS has failed to develop recovery plans for many of the listed species, and some have been removed from the list because they are now extinct!

A logger prepares to drop a 300-year-old western hemlock in the Olympic National Forest.

Why Old-Growth Timber?

FORESTS provide lumber for buildings and furniture, and pulp wood for paper products. Some of the lumber is obtained from trees on plantations—huge "tree farms" where young trees grown from seeds are set out at the right distance from one another and cared for until they are large enough to harvest. Often these trees are varieties specially bred for fast growth and resistance to disease. But old-growth timber, formed in the natural way over centuries, offers a higher quality of wood than that found in plantation trees. It is tight-grained, with fewer knots.

REQUEST FOR PROTECTED HABITAT

In 1974, wildlife researchers asked the federal government to set aside protected areas for spotted owls. It was estimated that at least 400 nesting pairs had to be protected so that there would be enough owls to continue the species, and each nesting pair would need at least 300 acres (120 hectares) of protected habitat to be able to find enough prey. The timber industry was outraged. Setting aside 120,000 acres (48,565 hectares) for the owls would be a loss of at least $10 billion in good timber. The proposal was rejected by the Forest Service and Bureau of Land Management, which called for more studies. This was the first of many delays.

WHO WOULD FIGHT FOR THE SPOTTED OWL?

Time passed, and nothing was being done about the spotted owl. By the early 1980s, many environmental groups often discussed the problem in their meetings and newsletters. The National Audubon Society, for example, formed an advisory panel to study the spotted owl in 1985. But even by 1987, most national groups were not prepared to fight for old-growth trees or spotted owls. The timber industry was just too big, and the general public had not heard much about the spotted owl.

In 1986, Canada listed the spotted owl as an endangered species. But in the United States, petitions by environmental groups to put the spotted owl on the endangered species list were denied. It took a lawsuit brought by the Sierra Club Legal Defense Fund to even get Congress to order an investigation of why the spotted owl was not being listed. Late in 1988, a Federal judge ruled that the U.S. Fish and Wildlife Service was violating

Exports are an important part of the timber industry.
Here logs from the Pacific Northwest have arrived in Japan.

the law, and in mid-1990 the FWS finally listed the northern spotted owl as a threatened species. ("Threatened" is not as serious a listing as endangered, but it provides protection under federal law.) However, the government still was not doing anything to protect the spotted owl, and logging was proceeding as usual.

Meanwhile, environmental groups were using local lawsuits to fight for the old-growth forests and the spotted owl. Rulings by judges in Washington and Oregon held up sales of old-growth trees there, and a federal judge banned the sales on most federal lands until the government came up with a plan to protect the spotted owls. But Congress, still more concerned about logging jobs than about wildlife, passed a law prohibiting any court decisions from holding up logging. The environmental groups went back to the courts to fight the new law, and still the old-growth timber sales went on.

Are Lawsuits Necessary?

THE TIMBER industry complains that environmentalists should have gone through government channels rather than using lawsuits in their fight for the old-growth forests. But Andy Stahl of the Sierra Club Legal Defense Fund argues, "Trees were being cut at an incredible rate and it had to be stopped. . . . It's through lawsuits we've gotten the message out about old growth." Andy Kerr, conservation director of the Oregon National Resources Council, also believes that lawsuits are the best way to get the message across. In 1981, he filed the first appeal in the Northwest against a Forest Service timber sale, and by 1988, he was involved in 220 lawsuits in a single month. "We will do anything that's legal," he says.[2]

THE DEBATE CONTINUES

While the legal battles were raging, the general public was becoming more familiar with the spotted owl problem. At first, because national environmental groups had been hesitant to get involved with the fight, it was the smaller, more radical groups that drew media attention. Members of some of these groups attracted national TV coverage by tying themselves to trees, sabotaging logging equipment, and driving spikes into old-growth trees to prevent them from being cut. (The spikes don't hurt the trees but could damage logging equipment and thus prevent someone from cutting them. If you're having trouble picturing how this works, imagine a tree with a spiked collar.)

Slowly the media began to take notice of the plight of the spotted owl. Environmental magazines such as *Audubon* began writing about the old-growth forests and the spotted owl. Books were written urging protection of old-growth ecosystems. At first the media focused on the lawsuits that environmentalists brought against federal agencies that allowed logging of spotted owl habitats. But soon news reports began to reflect the larger issue of cutting down the old-growth forests.

Before long, the spotted owl had gained national attention. Eventually the spotted owl's plight was featured in *National Geographic*, and in June 1990, it made the cover of *Time* magazine. "The issue nationalized

In a 1989 protest, tree sitters—members of the environmental group Earth First!—took up posts in these giant evergreens to keep them from being cut.

much faster than I thought it would," comments Andy Kerr of the Oregon Natural Resources Council. "Fortunately, [the ancient forest is] a pretty ecosystem. If it was a grassland or a swamp it might have been harder."[3]

THE JACK WARD THOMAS COMMITTEE

Meanwhile, a committee made up of representatives from federal agencies, environmentalist groups, and industry had been formed in 1989 to decide what was needed to protect the spotted owl. The group was headed by Jack Ward Thomas, an Oregon biologist known for his work with elk.

When the committee's 427-page report was presented in 1990, it called for 7.7 million acres (3.1 million hectares) to be set aside for spotted owl habitat, including 3.1 million acres (1.3 million hectares) that earlier had been earmarked for loggers. The report declared that even with these efforts, up to half of the owl population would be lost over the next century. But never before had it been proposed to set aside so much land at such a huge economic cost for so few creatures.

The committee's report represented a new trend, in which scientific reasoning could help make decisions to reach a fair compromise between two competing interest groups. The panel realized that it would not be practical to try to save *all* the spotted owls. "Anyone who thinks you can put forward a conservation strategy that ignores the needs of people is crazy. It will fail. The spotted owl would have ended up with nothing," says Thomas.[4]

The committee found that the owls must have large areas of unbroken old growth in order to successfully mate and find prey. The conservation areas had to have at least half old-growth trees. The rest could be logged or second-growth trees. The Forest Service did not formally adopt the committee's recommendations, but it did stop tree sales in the habitat areas that were specified.

THE TIMBER GRIDLOCK

In 1991 the U.S. Fish and Wildlife Service came out with its own proposal, as it had been ordered to do by a Federal Court judge. This plan called for a protected area of 14 million acres (5.7 million hectares). That was nearly double the compromise amount recommended by the Jack Ward Thomas Committee, and it set off a new storm of arguments.

While the arguments raged, Federal Judge William Dwyer in Seattle banned the sale of timber from all owl and old-growth habitat in national forests until federal agencies came up with an acceptable plan to protect the spotted owl. Judge Dwyer scolded the federal agencies for their years of stalling, in clear violation of environmental laws. He pointed out that protecting the owl would not affect the economies of Washington, Oregon, and California to a large extent, because the logging industry provided only a small percentage of the jobs in the Pacific Northwest. And even if some jobs were lost, preserving the wilderness would make the area more desirable for new industries and workers.

By 1992 the Forest Service was hoping to end the court order by adopting the Jack Ward Thomas Committee recommendations. Observers found it amusing that the timber industry and government were now willing to set aside 7.7 million acres (3.1 million hectares) of land to protect the owl. How much people's attitudes had changed!

Now timber sales were stopped on the federal lands, but logging still went on. Some of the trees that were cut had already been sold to the

With caps and shirts advertising their views, loggers rally
to show opposition to restrictions on their industry.

timber industry several years before. And many private landowners continued to sell off their trees. In Oregon, in fact, loggers went from door to
door urging landowners to have their trees cut before stricter environmental laws were passed and while the prices were still high. By 1993, so
much was being cut that observers began describing the situation as the
"Timber Rush of '93"!

Salmon Are in Danger, Too

THE NORTHWEST salmon industry is near collapse. Logging has polluted streams so that, according to the American Fisheries Society, 101 of the 214 native salmon stocks in the Pacific Northwest are in danger of extinction. In 1988, $1.25 billion was generated from sport and commercial salmon fishing. By 1992, that figure had fallen to $200 million. (By comparison, timber brings in $15 billion.)

In the spring of 1991, four subspecies of salmon that migrate from the ocean to Idaho to spawn were declared either endangered or threatened. This opened the door for numerous listings of Pacific Northwest salmon. Unlike the spotted owl, salmon is an important source of income for the Northwest. So the spotted owl may get some help as more powerful interests fight to keep its habitat intact in order to protect the salmon.

Salmon travel from the ocean to fresh water to spawn, or lay their eggs.

THE OWL-VERSUS-JOBS DEBATE

The timber industry complains that protecting the spotted owl costs jobs for people. In 1992, the U.S. Fish and Wildlife Service estimated that by 1995, more than 32,000 jobs would be lost due to spotted owl protection. Only half as much timber was harvested in 1992 as in 1989, before the spotted owl was declared threatened. In addition, as the production of lumber decreased, its price went up dramatically. That, in turn, increased the cost of new houses and other buildings.

Actually, though, it's not fair to blame the spotted owl for all the logging jobs lost. Since the mid-1970s, the timber industry has introduced efficient new machinery in its lumber mills, and robots have

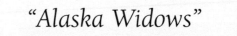

"Alaska Widows"

WHEN LOGGING is stopped in an old-growth forest, it's not just the loggers who are laid off. Truckers and mill workers are out of jobs, too, and the stores and businesses that served their community begin to fail. In one of these endangered logging towns, Oakridge, Oregon, some families have lost their homes and are forced to live in tents and get their meals from community food banks. Some Oakridge loggers now work in Alaska to earn the money to save their homes. They are separated from their families for ten months a year. The wives who are left behind call themselves "Alaska Widows."

replaced many human workers. In Washington, for example, the same amount of timber was cut in 1986 as in 1976, but by 15,000 fewer workers. Moreover, increasing exports of raw, unfinished logs to other countries, such as Japan, have eliminated many lumber-related jobs in the United States. (In the late 1980s, one quarter of all the timber cut in Oregon and Washington was shipped overseas as whole logs.)

A timber industry practice has helped to wipe out logging jobs in some areas. Before World War II, trees were selectively cut. But in the late 1960s *clearcutting* (cutting down every tree on a logging site) was adopted because it was more economically efficient. Between Eric Forsman's sighting of a spotted owl in 1968 and the government's acknowledgment that the spotted owl is threatened with extinction, more than a million acres (400,000 hectares) of old growth were cut. But once a forest has been clearcut, the trees are gone, and it will take years—even centuries—to replace them.

Ironically, this industry practice has led to a backlash and helped to strengthen the support for conservation efforts. A clearcut area looks barren and ugly. The sight of it, looking like a wound gouged out in the surrounding forest, shocks people and makes them think.

THE TIMBER SUMMIT OF 1993

In the spring of 1993, President Bill Clinton held a "forest summit" to try to end the timber problems in the Pacific Northwest. Environmentalists and the timber industry got a chance to voice their opinions. A few months later President Clinton presented his plan to "break the logjam."

The timber industry was not happy with the President's plan because it called for cutting two-thirds less timber than the level cut during the

It will take many years for new trees to grow in this clearcut.

1980s. However, this was the same amount of timber that was being cut 50 years earlier, and scientists had warned then that this natural resource would run out in a relatively short time at that pace. Environmentalists weren't happy with the President's plan, either, because there would not be any large, formal wilderness areas. Seven million acres (2.8 million hectares), about 80 percent of the nation's remaining forests, would be set aside as reserve areas, but selective logging would be allowed.

Clearcuts— Getting a Clear View

BECAUSE clearcutting looks so devastating, timber companies and the Forest Service leave a strip of trees along highways to prevent people from seeing the clearcuts. As the debate over old-growth forests grew heated, environmentalists sought out the help of Project Lighthawk, a group of volunteer pilots, to fly media and public officials over heavily logged areas in the Pacific Northwest to show how barren and eroded clearcuts are. One of the pilots, George Atiyeh, says, "I firmly believe if we could get everyone in Washington and Oregon into the air to see this logging, it would stop tomorrow."[5] Atiyeh once was part-owner of a timber company and a sawmill. But flying over the areas he had logged made him see things differently. He gave up the timber business and became an active environmentalist. "I didn't want to be responsible for the destruction of the last old-growth forests," he says.[6] The logging industry claims that the view from the air is misleading. They say they are replanting six trees for every one harvested. But environmentalists point out that it takes hundreds of years to re-establish a forest.

President Bill Clinton talks with participants at the 1993 "forest summit."

Biologists were concerned because salvage logging (harvesting of dead wood) was to be allowed under the Clinton plan. Both the spotted owl and its favorite prey, such as flying squirrels and wood rats, use dead trees and brush for nesting areas. Insects that live in the fallen trees help to break down the dead matter and recycle valuable nutrients for the forest growth. But wildlife expert Jack Ward Thomas points out that moderate salvaging reduces the risk of fire and tree disease.

The President's plan would help save the salmon, too. It called for protecting streams and watersheds in the old-growth forest areas. In addition, $1.2 billion in aid would be set aside for economic development and for retraining logging industry workers. Some out-of-work loggers would be put to work restoring damaged streams.

HELP FOR OWLS AND LOGGING

President Clinton wanted to show that we can protect the owls and keep the timber industry, too. The logging just can't be done as fast as it has been. Forest experts say that at the current rate of harvesting in the Northwest, all old-growth forests outside wilderness areas will disappear in two to three decades. Then there wouldn't be any more big trees to cut. "The spotted owl and the old-growth logger are endangered for the same reason—they're running out of habitat," says George Atiyeh.[7]

Selective cutting instead of clearcutting helps preserve forests; trees are healthier when not crowded too closely. It also creates additional jobs because it is more time-consuming than clearcutting. So preserving the spotted owl's ecosystem will actually help to keep the timber industry going and create more jobs for loggers in the long run.

THE BROADER PICTURE

Timber is no longer the driving force behind the economies of the Pacific Northwest. Less than 10 percent of the nation's building lumber comes from federal forests in the Northwest. In Oregon and Washington, 30,000 timber jobs had been lost over a ten-year period, but 932,000 other jobs were gained.

The overall economy of the Pacific Northwest may not have been affected by the loss of logging jobs, but for many individuals their whole world has changed. Some logging communities are just too far out of the way for tourist or other industries to provide enough jobs for the whole town.

A joint study by the Forest Service and Bureau of Land Management predicted a gloomy future. The report concluded that in the communities hardest hit by the loss of timber-related jobs, many social problems could be expected, such as increased cases of violence, family abuse, divorce, delinquency, vandalism, alcoholism, and suicide. The problem is more than financial; it is a cultural issue, too. "This is what we do. We want to do it as long as we can, and we want our kids to do it," says Harry Hershey, founder of an Oregon group called Save Our Sawmills.[8]

The spotted owl touched off a nationwide debate on the future of the national forests. Here, protesters march at the Capitol in Washington, D.C.

LEARNING TO ADAPT

Other communities are much more optimistic, and many are successfully moving toward an economy based on tourism, recreation, and high technology. In Oakridge, Oregon, for example, where 1,000 timber jobs were lost, the town has made efforts to attract tourists and businesses.

The economic aid that President Clinton's plan calls for should make it easier for many communities to adjust. Other policies can help provide more jobs in the timber-processing industry. For example, exporting logs to Japan takes jobs away from American millworkers. In 1990, Congress banned the exporting of unprocessed logs from most state lands. (It was already banned on federal lands.) Exports of timber from private lands continued, though. In 1992 more lumber from private land was exported than was cut from all of the national forests in the Northwest. New regulations could greatly decrease this loss of resources.

A CHANGE IN ATTITUDES: THE IMPORTANCE OF BIODIVERSITY

As William Dietrich points out in *The Final Forest*, the battle for the spotted owl illustrates that there has been a shift from concern only for animals that people are familiar with to the idea that these familiar animals are linked to a whole web of diverse animals and plants.

In the past, a top priority of government forest and wildlife agencies was to provide game for hunters and trappers. Wildlife departments used to be called "game departments." Little attention was given to other

A Life-and-Death Dilemma

MEDICAL SCIENCE added a new complication to the spotted owl controversy. In 1963, researchers testing various plant chemicals discovered that *taxol*, a substance from the bark of yew trees, stopped cancer cells from multiplying in laboratory cultures. In the 1980s tests on a few human cancer patients were begun. Taxol treatments made tumors shrink in a number of patients with advanced breast, ovarian, and lung cancer. The National Cancer Institute wanted to test the new drug on larger numbers of patients. But this posed a cruel dilemma. Taxol is present in several types of yews, but its main source is the Pacific yew (the spotted owl's favorite summer roost). Although there are close to 30 million Pacific yew trees scattered among the old-growth forests of Washington and Oregon, it takes the bark of six 100-year-old trees to treat a single patient. About 38,000 yews had to be cut for just the first year of large-scale testing. Yews grow so slowly that even with careful, selective cutting and replanting, the needs of the world's cancer patients would use up the whole supply very quickly. And cutting the Pacific yews would disturb the spotted owl's habitat. Research groups around the world began efforts to extract taxol from yew needles instead of bark, and to make taxol in the laboratory. In the early 1990s, several teams of chemists announced their success. Although taxol's benefits are still uncertain, it is hoped that the new synthetic drugs will help cancer patients without having to disturb the old-growth forests.

wildlife species. Professors taught that old-growth forests were "biological deserts" because big game animals did not live there. Clearcuts were seen as good because the brush that grew up on the land allowed deer and elk to move in. The land was viewed simply in terms of what recreational or industrial use it could be put to.

While environmentalists were certainly concerned about the fate of the northern spotted owl when they fought for its survival, many saw this battle as an opportunity to save more than just the spotted owl. The spotted owl was just one of many creatures that lived in the ecosystem of

Let's not forget the Mexican spotted owl

WITH ALL the talk about the northern spotted owl, much less attention has been paid to the Mexican spotted owl. It is smaller than its cousins, about 17 inches (43 centimeters) long. It is an ashy chestnut-brown with large white spots, and a yellow to ivory beak. Mexican spotted owls eat wood rats and other small rodents, but they catch more insects than their northern cousins.

Mexican spotted owls are found mostly in Arizona and New Mexico, but their range is from central Colorado and Utah south into southern Mexico. These owls live mainly in mixed old-growth forests with steep, well-shaded, rocky canyons. Logging may soon be changing about three quarters of the suitable owl habitat in New Mexico and Arizona.

Like the northern spotted owl, the Mexican spotted owl is an indicator species for old-growth forests, and it, too, is threatened with extinction. In 1993, it was officially listed as threatened.

Wildflowers and mosses carpet the floor of this ancient forest. The spotted owl is just one of many rare and wonderful living things in the complex old-growth ecosystem.

the old-growth forests. But it was the perfect animal to lead the battle to save old growth because it is an attractive animal, and it is in danger. It was easy to get the public interested because people are usually most sympathetic to attractive animals. And people like to root for underdogs, especially when they have a chance to win. It isn't too late to save the spotted owl, if we stop the cutting of old-growth forests now. And if we do, salmon, flying squirrels, martens, and many more forest species will be saved, too.

The spotted owl has also become a symbol of the whole fight for the world's endangered species. Every day, whole species become extinct because of human activities. Many people think that we have a responsibility to protect endangered species—especially those that are endangered because of us. They feel that something important is lost each time a species disappears. Some believe that these species have just as much right to live on our planet as we do. Others point out that we cannot predict what priceless resources—like the cancer drug taxol found in the bark of yew trees—might be lost if we continue unthinkingly to use and waste our planet's resources. The widely publicized debate over the fate of the spotted owl has helped make people think about such questions and realize that economic development must work hand in hand with preserving nature.

NOTES

1. William Dietrich, *The Final Forest*
(New York: Simon & Schuster, 1992), p. 82.

2. Dietrich, p. 222.

3. Dietrich, p. 214.

4. Dietrich, p. 227.

5. Dietrich, p. 114.

6. Seth Zuckerman, *Saving Our Ancient Forests*
(Los Angeles: Living Planet Press, 1991), p. 34.

7. Zuckerman, p. 52.

8. Zuckerman, p. 56.

FACTS ABOUT THE SPOTTED OWL

Height (or length)	16 to 19 inches (41 to 48 centimeters) in length
Weight	Males weigh up to 1½ pounds (about 1 kilogram); females weigh a few ounces more
Color	Rich, chocolate-brown color with white spots on top of head and back of neck
Food	Squirrels, young snowshoe hares, pocket gophers, deer mice, wood rats, bats, shrews, moles, small birds such as Steller's jays, small owls, frogs, and insects
Reproduction	Breed every other year starting with the third year; lay 1 to 4 eggs (usually 2)
Care for young	Female sits on the eggs nearly full time, and the male brings food to her; male continues to bring food to female up to two weeks after eggs are hatched; both parents feed the young until they can hunt on their own
Range	Western side of North America, from southwestern British Columbia down to central Mexico (northern spotted owl from British Columbia to northern California)
Population size	3,000 to 5,000 pairs
Social behavior	Usually mate for life except for winter when the pair separate and each lives alone; return to the same nest each spring
Life span	15 years

FURTHER READING

Dietrich, William. *The Final Forest.*
New York: Simon & Schuster, 1992.

Gallant, Roy A. *Earth's Vanishing Forests.*
New York: Macmillan, 1992.

Selsam, Millicent, and Joyce Hunt.
A First Look at Owls, Eagles, and Other Hunters of the Sky.
New York: Walker, 1986.

Siy, Alexandra. *Ancient Forests.*
New York: Macmillan, 1991.

Zuckerman, Seth. *Saving Our Ancient Forests.*
Los Angeles: Living Planet Press, 1991.

ORGANIZATIONS TO CONTACT

Defenders of Wildlife
1244 19th Street, NW
Washington, DC 20036
(202) 659-9510

EarthWatch
680 Mt. Auburn Street, P.O. Box 403N
Watertown, MA 02272
(617) 926-8200

Environmental Defense Fund
257 Park Avenue
New York, NY 10010

Hawk Watch International
P.O. Box 35706
Albuquerque, NM 87176
(505) 255-7622

National Audubon Society
700 Broadway
New York, NY 10003
(212) 979-3000

National Wildlife Federation
1412 16th Street, NW
Washington, DC 20036
(202) 797-6800

The Nature Conservancy
1815 N. Lynn St.
Arlington, VA 22209
(703) 841-5300

Rocky Mountain Raptor Program
Veterinary Teaching Hospital, Colorado State University
300 W. Drake
Fort Collins, CO 80523
(303) 491-0398

Sierra Club
730 Polk Street
San Francisco, CA 94109
(415) 776-2211

Sutton Avian Research Center
P.O. Box 2007
Bartlesville, OK 74005

U.S. Fish and Wildlife Service
Publications Unit
Washington, DC 20240

The Wilderness Society
P.O. Box 296
Federalsburg, MD 21632
(202) 833-2300

Wildlands Studies
3 Mosswood Circle
Cazadero, CA 95421
(707) 632-5665

INDEX

Page numbers in *italics* refer to illustrations.

Alaska Widows, 42
Ancient Fisheries Society, 41
Ancient forests, 9–12, *11*, 18, 28–29, 32, 35, 36, 38, 43, 47, 51, 52
Atiyeh, George, 45, 47
Audubon magazine, 36

Barrel owls, 15, 23
Breeding, 21
Bureau of Land Management, 12, 30, 33, 48

California spotted owls, 15, *16*, 21
Canaries, 10
Cancer, 51, 54
Clearcutting, 43, *44*, 45, 52
Clinton, Bill, 43, 45–47, *46*, 50

Dietrich, William, 28, 50
Douglas fir, 17

Dwyer, William, 39

Ecosystem, 10, 52
Endangered Species Act of 1973, 30–31
Environmentalists, 10, 12, 29, 33, 35, 36, 38, 45, 52
Exports of timber, 43, 50
Extinction, 31, 52, 54

Facial disk, 13
Final Forest, The (Dietrich), 28, 50
Flying squirrels, 19, 29, 46
Forest Service, 12, 28, 30, 33, 39, 45, 48
Forest summit (1993), 43, 45, 46, *46*
Forsman, Eric, 24, 26, 30

Great horned owls, 23

Hemlock, 17
Hershey, Harry, 48
Hoot owls, 15

Indicator species, 10, 52
Interior, Department of the, 12

Jack Ward Thomas Committee, 38–39
Job-versus-owl debate, 10, 12, 15, 36,
    38–40, 42–43

Kerr, Andy, 35, 38

Logging, 9–12, 15, 23, 29, *32*, 35, 36,
    38–40, 42–43, *44*, 45, 47, 48, 50,
    52

Mexican spotted owls, 15, 52
Mill workers, 42, 50

National Audubon Society, 33
National Geographic magazine, 36
Northern spotted owls, 15
    declining population of, 9, 11, 23
    habitat, 17–19, *18*, 28–29, 46, 51
    hunting by, 10, 13, *14*, 19
    job-versus-owl debate, 10, 12, 15,
        36, 38–40, 42–43
    life cycle of, 21, 23
    owlets, 21, *22*, 23
    sight and hearing of, 13
    sounds of, 15, 17, 26
    spotting, 24, *25*, 26, 28
    as threatened species, 35

Oakridge, Oregon, 42, 50
Old-growth forests, 9–12, *11*, 18, 28–
    29, 32, 35, 36, 38, 43, 47, 51, 52
Oregon Natural Resources Council, 11
Organizations, 59–60

Overstory, 19
Owlets, 21, 22, 23

Pacific yew, 19, 51
Pellets, 26
Plantation trees, 32
Project Lighthawk, 45

Redwoods, 11, 17, 28

Salmon, 41, 47
Salvage logging, 46
Save Our Sawmills, 48
Selective logging, 45, 47, 51
Sequoias, 12
Sierra Club Legal Defense Fund, 33
Spotted owls (*see* California spotted
    owls; Mexican spotted owls;
    Northern spotted owls)
Stahl, Andy, 35

Taxol, 51, 54
Thomas, Jack Ward, 38, 46
Timber industry, 29, 33, *34*, 35, 39,
    42–43, 45, 47, 48, 50
Time magazine, 36
Tree sitters, 36, *37*
Truckers, 42

Understory, 19
U.S. Fish and Wildlife Service, 31, 33,
    35, 39, 42

Wood rats, 46

Yew trees, 19, 51, 54

ABOUT THE AUTHORS

Alvin Silverstein is a
professor of biology at the
City University of New York,
College of Staten Island;
Virginia Silverstein, his wife,
is a translator of Russian scientific literature. Together they
have published nearly 100 books
on science and health topics.

Robert Silverstein joined his
parents' writing team in 1988
and has since co-authored more
than a dozen books with them,
including the Food Power! nutrition
series from The Millbrook Press.